BLAST OFF!™

on

New Jersey Writing

Book 4

Buckle Down
PUBLISHING COMPANY

ISBN 0-7836-1660-6

Catalog #BF NJ4W 1   2 3 4 5 6 7 8 9 10

Cover art: Images © 1996 PhotoDisc, Inc.

TABLE OF CONTENTS

Appendix

Introduction

Writing Makes Things Happen

Do you remember the first time you ever wrote a story on your own? If you do, you probably remember what a thrill it was to see your ideas on paper. When you're the writer, *you* are the person who makes things happen.

Put a Genie in Your Soda Pop Can

When you write, you can do all sorts of things that aren't possible in real life. You can sail around the world. You can visit with aliens from outer space. You can even put a genie in your soda pop can.

Writing can help you do other things, too. You can share your thoughts and feelings with your best friend. You can pour out your joys and disappointments in a secret journal. You can ask for things you need or want, like a bigger allowance.

Anything that you can say, feel, or imagine, you can put into words on paper.

Get Ready, Get Set, Go!

This book will help you write about whatever is important to you. It will also help you do your best writing in school. All *you* have to do is work through the book with your teacher and then practice what you learn.

One day you'll take a state writing test. Everything you learn as you work through this book will help you do your best on the test. By the time you're done, you'll think of the test as a chance to show off your writing skills.

Count Down to Blast Off!

It's easier to feel that you've really done something if you keep track of your progress. When you finish an assignment in this book, write down the date you finished. Then have your teacher initial the entry. Each assignment you complete will be one more step toward becoming a better writer.

Date	Practice Assignment Completed	Teacher's Initials
	Lesson 1: Understanding the Topic	
_____	Prewriting Activity (pg. 7)	_____
_____	Writing Assignment (pg. 8)	_____
	Lesson 2: Getting Ideas	
_____	Prewriting Activity 1 (pg. 9)	_____
_____	Prewriting Activity 2 (pg. 10)	_____
_____	Prewriting Activity 3 (pg. 11)	_____
_____	Writing Assignment (pg. 12)	_____
	Lesson 3: Organizing a Report	
_____	Practice Activity (pg. 14)	_____
_____	Prewriting Activity (pg. 15)	_____
_____	Writing Assignment (pg. 16)	_____
	Lesson 4: Organizing a Story	
_____	Prewriting Activity (pg. 18)	_____
_____	Writing Assignment (pg. 19)	_____
	Lesson 5: The Nuts and Bolts of Poetry	
_____	Prewriting Activity 1 (pg. 23)	_____
_____	Practice Activity (pg. 24)	_____
_____	Prewriting Activity 2 (pg. 25)	_____
_____	Prewriting Activity 3 (pg. 26)	_____
_____	Writing Assignment (pg. 28)	_____
	Lesson 6: It's Your Voice	
_____	Writing Assignment 1 (pg. 30)	_____
_____	Prewriting Activity (pg. 31)	_____
_____	Writing Assignment 2 (pg. 32)	_____
_____	Prewriting Activity (pg. 32)	_____
	Lesson 7: Word Choice	
_____	Practice Activity (pg. 34)	_____

Prewriting

Give Yourself a Running Start

If you wanted to jump as far and as well as you could, how would you do it? Would you stand still and just *jump*? Or would you warm up a little, think about what you were going to do, then take a running start?

If you want to *write* as well as you can, you usually need to warm up a little, too. Prewriting is a way to give yourself a running start.

Before you can write, you need something to write about. You also need to organize your ideas so that they make sense.

Prewriting is what you do before you write. Prewriting activities can help you get ideas for a topic or figure out what to do with a topic that's been assigned to you. In addition, prewriting can help you make sense of the ideas you have about a topic.

You've Got to Light a Fire Before You Can Blast Off!

You can "light a fire" by doing prewriting activities before you start to write. There are many different prewriting activities to choose from. First, we will look at things you can do when you are assigned a topic by your teacher. Then we will look at ways to come up with ideas about a topic, whether it is your teacher's topic or your own. Once you're ready to write, even gravity won't hold you down!

Lesson 1

Understanding the Topic

When you're given a writing assignment, it is important that you understand the topic. If you don't, you may write about the wrong topic, like the student in the cartoon.

Let's pretend that your science teacher wants you to write a report. This is what she tells you:

> *This week we will be studying the Amazon Rain Forest. You will choose an animal from that area to write about. Find out all that you can about where the animal lives, what it eats, and any other interesting facts. The purpose of this report is to tell your classmates as much as you can about the animal you choose.*

Before you start, you need to understand the topic. Write the answers to the following questions on the lines provided.

1. Why am I writing?

   _____

2. Who am I writing to?

   _____

3. What am I writing about?

   _____

4. What kind of writing is it (such as a letter, story, poem, etc.)?

   _____

Any time you are given a writing topic, answer these four questions first. They'll help you get started in the right direction.

Prewriting Activity

Understanding the Topic

Directions: Read the topic below. Then answer the questions that follow.

Topic: You and your best friend are planning a costume party. Everyone in your class is invited, except for Margo, a new girl at school. Neither you nor your friend know Margo. You want to write a letter introducing the two of you and inviting her to the party.

1. Why am I writing?

    _____

2. Who am I writing to?

    _____

3. What am I writing about?

    _____

4. What kind of writing is it (such as a letter, story, poem, etc.)?

    _____

Writing Assignment
Understanding the Topic

Directions: Use the space below to write a letter to Margo.

_____

_____

_____

_____

_____

_____

_____

_____

_____

_____

_____

_____

_____

_____

_____

_____

_____

_____

_____

_____

_____

_____

Lesson 2

Getting Ideas

You might not have any trouble coming up with topics to write about. But figuring out what to say once you have a topic can be as difficult as pulling your own teeth. It doesn't have to be that hard. The following activities will give you some practice coming up with ideas about a topic.

Using Literature to Get Ideas

Sometimes reading someone else's writing will help you get ideas for your own writing. In this section, you will read a poem to get ideas for a story of your own.

Prewriting Activity 1

Getting Ideas

Directions: Read along silently in your workbook as your teacher reads the following poem aloud to you. The poem is about cats. As you listen to the poem, try to picture the cats in your mind.

Making Mischief
by Jordan Ratliff

I named my kitten Mischief
because I thought the name was cute.
Now Mischief has become
a grown-up furry troublemaker.

What if I had named her Peaceful?
Would she purr softly,
content to stare out the window
or just cuddle up with me?

Mischief's brother's name is Astro,
like the dog in a cartoon show.
Now Astro's owners say he's acting
like a real "space cadet."

What if they'd named him Einstein?
Would he be a brighter cat
who'd know enough to find his home
and come in out of the rain?

Jeni's cat is named *Maigri*.
His name means "chief" in Zarma.
He thinks he is the boss of Jeni's house.
He welcomes whom he pleases
    and hisses at the rest.

What if she had named him *Bolita*,
which means "little ball" in Spanish?
Would he bounce around her house
or roll across the room to entertain
    her guests?

I know I'll never name a kitten Tiger.
He might chase me through the kitchen
and try to catch my toes
for his afternoon snack.

Cats should come with warning labels:
"The name you give to me
will tell me who I should become.
Choose wisely, or beware!"

Drawing a Picture to Get Ideas

Sometimes drawing a picture can help you come up with ideas. Let's give it a try.

Prewriting Activity 2
Getting Ideas

Directions: To help you get ready to write your own story, think about a pet you've had or someone else's pet you've known. Look back at the poem and read it again. Then draw a picture of the pet you will write about and tell its name.

A Pet Named _____

Now tell some things about the pet in the picture.

_____

_____

_____

_____

_____

Using a Graphic Organizer to Get Ideas

You read a poem to help you think of ideas. Then you drew a picture of the pet you wish to write about. Now let's go one step further.

Prewriting Activity 3

Getting Ideas

Directions: Answer the questions on the lines provided. The answers you give will help you write your own story. Remember, this prewriting activity is just to help you. It will not be scored.

A PET NAMED

What kind of animal is this pet?

Whose pet is it?

What is special about this pet?

What does this pet like to do?

How do you feel about this pet?

Do you want to say anything else about this pet?

Does this pet's name fit? Why or why not?

Writing Assignment
Getting Ideas

Directions: You have used three different types of prewriting activities to gather ideas about a pet. Now use your ideas to write a paragraph about the pet you chose.

_____

_____

_____

_____

_____

_____

_____

_____

_____

_____

_____

_____

_____

_____

_____

_____

Lesson 3

Organizing a Report

When you are coming up with ideas, don't stop the flow of your thoughts. Think of as many ideas as you can. Let one idea lead to another, and another, and another. . . . Just make sure to write down those ideas.

Once you have gathered your ideas, decide which ones you want to keep. Then organize your ideas. There are many different ways to organize ideas. This section will show you one way to organize reports.

Linking Your Train of Thought

Just as a train needs an engine, cars, and a caboose, your writing needs a beginning, a middle, and an end. When you write a report, your "train of thought" might look like this:

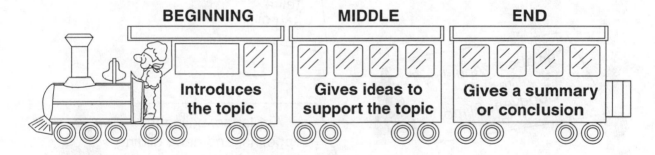

BEGINNING	MIDDLE	END
Introduces the topic	Gives ideas to support the topic	Gives a summary or conclusion

For example, imagine that you are asked to write a report about something that could be done to care for the earth. You decide to write about recycling. Here is one way you might organize your report.

Recycle to Save the Earth

BEGINNING • Introduce my topic. • Tell why my topic is interesting.	Tell what recycling is. Tell that recycling can help with many problems in our environment.
MIDDLE • Give ideas to support my topic. • Give details about the ideas.	**Idea:** Tell how recycling helps with the problems of too much trash and pollution. **Idea:** Tell how recycling helps save resources. **Idea:** Tell how recycling is easy for people to do.
END • Briefly summarize my topic and the most important points.	Tell why it is a good idea to recycle.

Practice Activity

Organizing a Report

Directions: Nate is writing a report on flying machines. Below are the ideas he has for writing his report. Help him organize his report by drawing a line connecting each idea to the part of the train it should go with.

Flying High

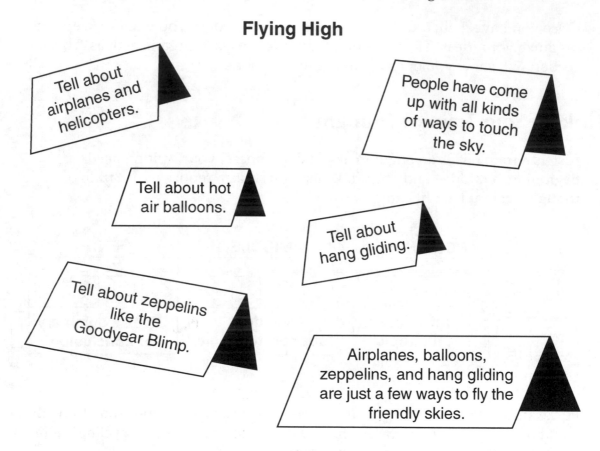

Tell about airplanes and helicopters.

People have come up with all kinds of ways to touch the sky.

Tell about hot air balloons.

Tell about hang gliding.

Tell about zeppelins like the Goodyear Blimp.

Airplanes, balloons, zeppelins, and hang gliding are just a few ways to fly the friendly skies.

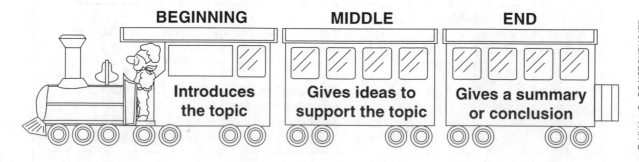

BEGINNING — Introduces the topic

MIDDLE — Gives ideas to support the topic

END — Gives a summary or conclusion

Prewriting Activity

Organizing a Report

Directions: For this activity, you will plan a report about an endangered species. You might choose from the following animals:

orangutan   cheetah   red wolf
crocodile   black rhinoceros   tiger
blue whale   snow leopard   Indian elephant

You may use an encyclopedia or other resources to find information on these or other endangered species. Use the chart below to gather and organize ideas for your report.

The endangered species I will write about is _____ .

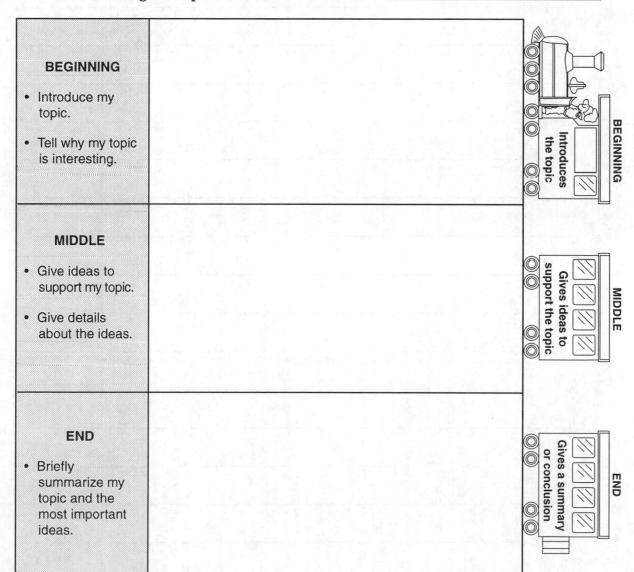

Writing Assignment
Organizing a Report

Directions: Now use the ideas you gathered on page 15 to write a brief report on an endangered species. Your report should have a beginning, a middle, and an end.

_____

_____

_____

_____

_____

_____

_____

_____

_____

_____

_____

_____

_____

_____

_____

_____

_____

Organizing a Story

When you write a story, you also need to have a beginning, a middle, and an end. Here is what your "train of thought" might look like for a made-up story.

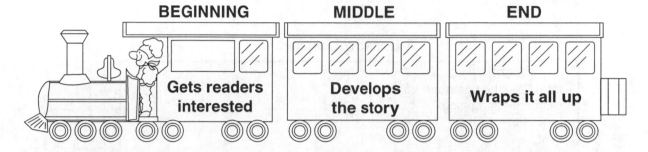

Let's look at how this works in an easy story most of us know.

Goldilocks and the Three Bears

BEGINNING	
• Introduce the characters.	Mama Bear, Papa Bear, Baby Bear, and Goldilocks
• Describe the setting.	a little house in the woods
• Hint at the trouble.	Goldilocks goes into someone's house, and she shouldn't be there.
MIDDLE	
• Show the characters talking and doing things.	Goldilocks talks to herself, "This chair is too hard," and so on.
• Show the characters' problems.	Goldilocks falls asleep in the bed that is "just right." Meanwhile, the three bears start for home.
• Show the characters' feelings.	The three bears are puzzled and a little cranky to find that someone has been eating their porridge and sitting in their chairs.
• Hint at how the problems will be solved.	The bears go upstairs and will soon find Goldilocks asleep.
END	
• Show how the problems are solved.	Goldilocks wakes up to see three bears staring at her. She runs all the way home.
• Show the characters' feelings.	Goldilocks is frightened by what has happened.
• Show how the characters are changed.	Goldilocks will never again go into strangers' homes uninvited. The three bears decide to keep their doors locked in the future.

Prewriting Activity

Organizing a Story

Directions: Think of an important lesson you have learned. Then imagine a story in which made-up characters learn the same important lesson. Use the chart below to gather and organize ideas for your story.

A Lesson Learned

BEGINNING • Introduce the characters. • Describe the setting. • Hint at the trouble.	
MIDDLE • Show the characters talking and doing things. • Show the characters' problems. • Show the characters' feelings. • Hint at how the problems will be solved.	
END • Show how the problems are solved. • Show the characters' feelings. • Show how the characters are changed.	

BEGINNING — Gets readers interested

MIDDLE — Develops the story

END — Wraps it all up

Writing Assignment
Organizing a Story

Directions: Use the ideas you gathered on page 18 to write a story of your own. Make sure your story has a beginning, a middle, and an end.

_____

_____

_____

_____

_____

_____

_____

_____

_____

_____

_____

_____

_____

_____

_____

_____

The Nuts and Bolts of Poetry

A poem is a wonderful way to express thoughts and feelings. It gives the writer a chance to be creative in ways that other types of writing might not allow. This lesson will teach you some tips about how to write poetry.

What Is a Poem?

Poetry can be quite different from **prose** (narrative or informational writing). Read the following selections. Think about how the selections are alike and how they are different as you read them.

Prose Passage

My Backyard
by Mary Dennison

Saturday was a beautiful day. There were a few clouds in the sky, but the sun was bright and warm. I decided to read a book while I sat outside. I leaned back in the patio chair and started to read. After a while, I grew tired of reading and just stared at the sky. The clouds were fluffy and white. They traveled across the sky, blocking the sun as they went.

Poem

clouds
by Michael Scheibach

clouds
play
leapfrog
with the sun
as I
watch and cheer
from
the empty grandstand
in the backyard

In what ways is the poem different from the prose passage?

_____

_____

_____

_____

_____

Poems have special features that make them different from prose:
- Poems often describe ordinary things in extraordinary ways.
- Poems often use "hard-working words" that appeal to the senses.
- Poems often contain unusual comparisons.
- Poems make every word count. They say as much as possible in as few words as possible.
- Poems are written in **lines** and **stanzas** rather than in sentences and paragraphs.

Some poems rhyme, but many do not.

Hard-Working Words

Choosing "hard-working words" is a key to good poetry. In each of the following examples, dull, lifeless words have been replaced with more lively ones. Notice how the new words paint a picture in the reader's mind.

> The autumn leaves *blew* around.
> The autumn leaves *whirled*, *skipped*, and *danced*.

> The smell of the perfume was *strong*.
> The *sticky*, *sweet* smell of the perfume filled every corner of the room.

When you write, use words that tell about sights, smells, sounds, tastes, and feelings. When you use verbs, choose verbs with *PUNCH!* Lively words can make your writing sparkle.

Prewriting Activity 1
Hard-Working Words

Directions: Imagine it is your birthday. You are sitting at a table. Your family has surprised you by serving your favorite meal. A plate has just been placed in front of you containing all your favorite foods. Close your eyes and imagine the sights and smells on the plate. Imagine how the food will taste. Imagine what the foods' textures are like. Then open your eyes and write a paragraph describing your "birthday meal." Try to use lively words in your description.

_____

_____

_____

_____

_____

_____

_____

_____

_____

_____

_____

_____

Comparisons

Poets often describe one thing by comparing it to another thing. Three types of comparisons poets use are called **similes, metaphors,** and **analogies.**

A **simile** uses the word *like* or *as* to compare two things. Here are some examples:

- The moon shines **like** a lantern.
- The clouds are **like** marshmallows.
- This bed is as hard **as** a rock.
- The water was as clear **as** a window pane.

A **metaphor** says that one thing actually *is* another. Here are a few examples:

- This bike is my magic carpet.
- These ants are tiny soldiers.
- We flew to New York in a silver bird.

An **analogy** is like the Energizer Bunny: It takes a simile or metaphor and keeps it going, and going, and going . . . Here is an example:

- **Metaphor:** The gravy was lava on my plate.
- **Analogy:** Gravy lava flowed from the mashed-potato volcano,
  and poured over the ridge of roast beef,
  oozed into the forest of spinach,
  covering every leaf.

Practice Activity

Comparisons

Directions: Complete the following similes. The first one has been done for you.

1. The panther is as black as *a moonless night*.

2. Young deer run as fast as _____

3. The raindrops sparkle like _____

4. Her dog sounds like _____

5. This sweater is as soft as _____

Directions: Describe the following items by using metaphors. The first one has been done for you.

6. The building is *an old, gray elephant* standing in the moonlight.

7. The crying baby is a _____

8. The wind is a _____

9. The stars are _____

10. A television set is _____

Prewriting Activity 2
Comparisons

Directions: Go back to the paragraph you wrote about your "birthday meal" (page 23). Choose one item you wrote about. Think of something you can compare that item to. Then write your comparison in the form of a simile on the line below.

1. A simile:

_____

Directions: Go back to the paragraph you wrote about your "birthday meal" (page 23). Choose one item you wrote about. Think of something you can compare that item to. Then write your comparison in the form of a metaphor on the line below.

2. A metaphor:

_____

Directions: Choose a simile or metaphor from the "birthday meal." You can choose one you wrote for numbers 1 or 2, or you can make up a new one. Then try to turn the simile or metaphor into an analogy.

3. An analogy:

_____

_____

Making Every Word Count

If you can cross out any word or phrase and not change the meaning of what you've written, do it! Look at this prose example:

> As I left my house and walked to school along the sidewalk, I looked over and I saw a kid I go to school with—my friend John—riding past me in some kind of a bus. (37 words)

Many words could be left out of this sentence without changing its meaning.

> As I ~~left my house and~~ walked to school ~~along the sidewalk, I looked over and~~ I saw ~~a kid I go to school with~~ —my friend John— riding ~~past me in some kind of~~ a bus. (13 words)

You can remove at least 24 words from the original sentence without changing its meaning. This kind of test should be used on each line of poetry. If you wanted to, you could take out even more words by rewriting the sentence like this:

> While walking to school, I saw my friend John riding a bus. (12 words)

The sentence has been shortened, but the key meaning has not changed. Of course, this sentence isn't poetry. But it is a good example of how to cut out extra words.

Prewriting Activity 3
Making Every Word Count

Directions: Go back to the paragraph you wrote about your "birthday meal" (page 23). Draw a line through any unnecessary words.

Lines and Stanzas

In a poem, a single idea can be written on a **line** all by itself. A sentence can be broken up into several lines.

Ideas that go together can be put into a **stanza.** Stanzas are the "paragraphs" of poetry.

Read the following poem. Notice how the ideas are organized into lines and stanzas.

Supperland
by Francis Williamson

Gravy lava flowed from the mashed-potato volcano,
and poured over the ridge of roast beef,
oozed into the forest of spinach,
covering every leaf.

Apples floated in a green Jello sea,
beneath a cloud of whipped cream,
and blueberry birds soared through the air
toward a bright melon sunbeam.

Writing Assignment

A Poem

Directions: Now you will write a poem. Your poem will be about your imaginary birthday meal. It can be rhymed or unrhymed. You may use the ideas you wrote on pages 23 and 25 to help you write your poem.

_____

_____

_____

_____

_____

_____

_____

_____

_____

_____

_____

_____

_____

_____

_____

_____

Drafting

Unit 1 was about the things you do before you write. You learned how to get ideas to write about. You also learned how to organize your ideas. Now what?

Putting Your Ideas on Paper

There are all kinds of ways to put your ideas on paper. What if you want to tell about a movie you just saw on videotape with your family? You could describe it in a letter to your best friend:

> Kenny,
>
> You really should see <u>Babe</u>. It's about a pig that herds sheep. It's awesome! The way the animals talk to each other is really cool...

You could write a report about the movie for your teacher at school.

> The movie <u>Babe</u> is about a pig that learns to herd sheep. My family and I really enjoyed this movie. The animals in the movie talk to each other, so it is easy to get to know them...

Or you could write about it in your secret journal.

> Mom, Dad, and I watched a movie tonight. We saw <u>Babe</u>. It was fun to spend the time together. I had a huge bowl of popcorn and soda...

You could describe the same event—watching a movie—in *three* different ways! With practice, you will be able to pick the best way to write what you want to say.

Lesson 6

It's Your Voice

Anything you can say out loud—or say to yourself—you can put on paper. In many ways, writing and talking are the same. If you try to write the same way you talk, writing can be easy. If you try to sound like someone else instead of yourself, your writing won't be as interesting to your readers.

You have only one voice. But you can use your voice many different ways. You can use it to make a serious speech to your class. You can use it to tell a silly joke to your friends. In both of these cases, your voice would probably sound different. The same is true when you write.

> We the people, in order to form a . . .

Who is Your Reader?

Sometimes the way you say things depends on who you're saying them to. You wouldn't talk to your principal in the same way you would talk to your best friend.

The next two activities will help you get a feel for the different ways you use your voice when you write. You will write two letters: one to a friend and one to a friend's parents.

Writing Assignment 1

A Letter to a Friend

Directions: Imagine that you went camping last weekend with your best friend's family. You went hiking, cooked over a campfire, and sang camp songs together. It was a lot of fun.

Topic: Write a letter to a different friend, not the one you went camping with. Tell this friend about the things you did on the camping trip. Use lots of details to describe the trip and how much fun you had.

Your letter should have the following parts:

- a **greeting,** like "Dear Kendra," or "Dear Joe,"
- a **body,** the part of the letter that says what you want to say
- a **closing,** like "Your friend," or "Sincerely,"

Also, be sure to **sign your name** at the bottom.

Prewriting Activity

A Letter to a Friend

1. Why am I writing?

    _____

2. Who am I writing to?

    _____

3. What am I writing about?

    _____

4. What kind of writing is it (such as a letter, story, poem, etc.)?

    _____

Directions: Write your letter on the lines below.

_____

_____

_____

_____

_____

_____

_____

_____

Writing Assignment 2

A Letter to Parents

Directions: Now write a letter to your best friend's parents to thank them for taking you on their camping trip. Tell them what you liked best about the trip. Thank them for taking you along.

Your letter should have the following parts:

- a **greeting,** like "Dear Mr. and Mrs. Smith,"
- a **body,** the part of the letter that says what you want to say
- a **closing,** like "Your friend," or "Sincerely,"

Also, be sure to **sign your name** at the bottom.

Prewriting Activity

A Letter to Parents

1. Why am I writing?

   _____

2. Who am I writing to?

   _____

3. What am I writing about?

   _____

4. What kind of writing is it (such as a letter, story, poem, etc.)?

   _____

Directions: Write your thank-you letter on the lines below.

_____

_____

_____

_____

_____

_____

_____

_____

_____

_____

_____

_____

_____

_____

_____

_____

Lesson 7

Word Choice

When you wrote to your friend, you probably used very different language than when you wrote to your best friend's parents. The letter to your friend is probably much more casual. It might contain slang. The letter to your friend's parents was probably much more formal.

A big part of writing is knowing what kind of language to use. More formal language is used for adults and people you don't know well. More casual language and slang is used for close family, good friends, or for writing to yourself. Stories often use casual language. Reports use formal language.

Casual, everyday language is easy to write. It's written just as we speak it. Formal language can be a bit harder. The next exercise will help you find ways to change casual language into more formal language.

Practice Activity

Word Choice

Directions: Rewrite the sentences below, changing the everyday language or slang into more formal language.

1. Tovia really **goofed up** when she forgot her paper route this morning.

   _____

2. Some kids **hang out** on the playground after school.

   _____

3. Alex got in trouble for **goofing off** during reading class.

   _____

4. We saw a really **cool** magic show last winter.

   _____

5. Hey, where are **you guys** going?

   _____

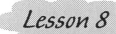 Lesson 8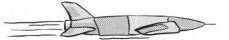

Details, Details, Details

Sometimes we write as if we were trying to get the job over with as soon as possible. We use general words that give very little information. Take this sentence for example:

> The boy ate a sandwich.

What boy? What kind of sandwich was it? Did he eat it a little at a time or in one huge bite? What if we said:

> The curly-haired nine-year-old boy took a huge bite out of the drippy jelly sandwich.

Now we have a much better picture.

 ## Practice Activity

Details

Directions: In the following exercise, help your readers paint a picture in their minds. Make the phrase on the left more interesting by using details to show your meaning. The first one has been done for you.

1. an animal   Sarah's small yellow kitten

2. a television show   _____

3. a book   _____

4. a family member   _____

5. a candy   _____

6. a person   _____

7. a sport   _____

8. something to drink   _____

9. a pair of pants   _____

10. a monster   _____

Writing Assignment

Details

Directions: On the lines below, use details to describe a famous person. Sounds easy? Well, there's a catch. You cannot tell the person's name.

Here are some tips for describing your famous person:

- What does the person look like?
- How does the person act?
- What is the person good at?
- What other things does the person do?

Write your description on the lines below.

_____

_____

_____

_____

_____

_____

_____

_____

_____

_____

Now let your teacher or another classmate read your description. Can they guess who you described?

Lesson 9

Sentences

Would you like to wear the same style of clothes every day of your life—the same kind of jeans, the same kind of shirt, the same kind of shoes . . . ? Sounds boring, doesn't it?

Sometimes writing can be like that. It's easy to use the same kinds of sentences all the time. That kind of writing just isn't very interesting, though.

Variety—It's the Spice of Life

A single idea can be expressed in many different ways. Imagine you are writing a story about an astronaut landing on an unknown planet. Think about how you could tell your readers the following things about the planet:

- The planet was covered with thick purple vines.
- The planet was hot and steamy.
- The planet was small.

You could write these three ideas in many different ways.

- Thick purple vines covered the small, hot, steamy planet.
- The planet was small, hot, and steamy, and it was covered with thick purple vines.
- Covering the small, hot, steamy planet were thick purple vines.

You'll have more fun writing when you use different kinds of sentences. And your readers will have more fun reading, too.

Practice Activity 1

Sentence Variety

Directions: Put each set of three sentences together into a new sentence or two. Then try to put the sentences together again in a different way.

1. Sam is my brother. He is younger than I am. He makes us all laugh.

   _____

   _____

   _____

   _____

2. My pet turtle is named Willow. Willow is as big as a dinner plate. She eats everything in sight.

   _____

   _____

   _____

3. Ruth is my best friend. We had fun last weekend. We went to the zoo together.

   _____

   _____

   _____

   _____

4. I made a puppet. It is a friendly monster. It smiles at kids.

   _____

   _____

   _____

Practice Activity 2

Sentence Variety

Directions: Read the following paragraph.

The swimming pool was in the park. The pool was big. Jody and Cassie were at the pool. Jody and Cassie were waiting in line. They were waiting for the diving board. A lot of people were at the pool. Cassie's turn came. Cassie walked to the end of the board. Cassie looked down. Cassie looked into the water. The water looked deep and scary. The water looked far away from the board. Cassie had never jumped from a diving board before.

Now, rewrite the paragraph so that the sentences have more variety. You may combine some of the sentences. You may put some of the sentences into your own words. You may choose to leave some of the sentences the way they are. You decide!

_____

_____

_____

_____

_____

_____

_____

_____

_____

_____

Lesson 10

Staying on Topic

Have you ever had a conversation like this?

> "Hey, Aaron. Wanna hear about a scary movie I saw on Saturday?"
> Lindsey asked.
> "Sure. I went to a ball game with Dale that day."
> "Really? I heard that Dale got a new puppy."
> "Yeah," Aaron said. "And Jan just got a pet parrot, like the ones in the
> zoo."
> "Cool! I like the birds in the zoo, especially the really bright, colorful
> ones."
> "Me, too. Oh . . . what were you saying about a movie?"

Remember when we talked about your "train of thought"? Sometimes your
train of thought can get off track. Getting off track may be fine when you're
talking, but it doesn't work very well in writing. When you write, you should
stick to the topic. The topic is the main idea you are talking about. Everything
you write should help your readers understand the topic.

Practice Activity

Staying on Topic

Directions: Read the paragraph below. The topic of the paragraph is
mosquito stings. Cross out any sentences that don't tell about mosquito
stings.

> Mosquitoes don't really bite, they sting. They don't have teeth and
> jaws like dogs. Dogs make good pets. Mosquitoes act like a nurse
> giving a shot. I had a shot one time when I was sick. It wasn't too bad.
> First, a mosquito spits out a substance that deadens a person's skin for
> a few seconds. Then it inserts a very fine needle-like stinger into the
> skin. This stinger is really skinny. It reminds me of a piece of very fine
> thread, like the thread my mom used to stitch up my torn shirt. When I
> tore that shirt, I was lucky I didn't get hurt. I should have been more
> careful. Anyway, through its stinger, a mosquito draws a tiny bit of
> blood from its victim. After the mosquito has eaten its fill, it removes
> its stinger. The victim doesn't start itching until the deadening has
> worn off.

Directions: Now rewrite the paragraph on mosquitoes, leaving out the sentences that aren't needed. You may put the paragraph in your own words if you like.

_____

_____

_____

_____

_____

_____

_____

Go back and reread the original paragraph. Which paragraph—yours or the original—will best help the reader understand how a mosquito goes about eating its lunch?

Lesson 11

Supporting the Topic

Liz is writing a letter to the editor of her school newspaper. She wants to say what she thinks about whether her school should make students wear uniforms. The first draft of her letter reads like this.

> Dear Editor,
>
> I think that school uniforms are a good idea. I hope the school board will *decide that we should wear them.*
>
> Sincerely,
>
> Liz Jurgens

We know Liz thinks that uniforms are a good idea. But why?

Just as a house needs walls to support the roof, your writing needs details to support the topic. Liz needs to tell us several reasons *why* she thinks uniforms are a good idea. Here are some reasons she might give:

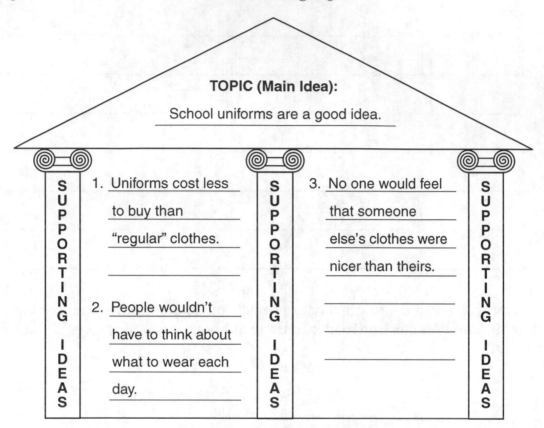

TOPIC (Main Idea):

School uniforms are a good idea.

SUPPORTING IDEAS

1. Uniforms cost less to buy than "regular" clothes.

2. People wouldn't have to think about what to wear each day.

SUPPORTING IDEAS

3. No one would feel that someone else's clothes were nicer than theirs.

SUPPORTING IDEAS

 Prewriting Activity

Supporting the Topic

Directions: Pretend your principal has decided that your school will have a "World Day." This day will celebrate the many different peoples who live in other countries.

Topic: Your principal has asked for ideas from students on ways to celebrate World Day. Some ideas are given below:

- **food fair** – a fair where foods from other countries are served

- **speaker's corner** – people who have moved to the United States from other countries come to speak at your school

- **dress-up day** – students come to school wearing clothes like those worn in other countries

- **music festival** – a festival where music from other countries is played

Directions: Pick the idea from page 42 that you like best, or come up with an idea of your own. Think of two or three reasons why the idea you picked would be a good way to celebrate World Day. Later, you will use your idea and reasons to write a letter to your principal.

Use the graphic organizer below to help you plan your letter.

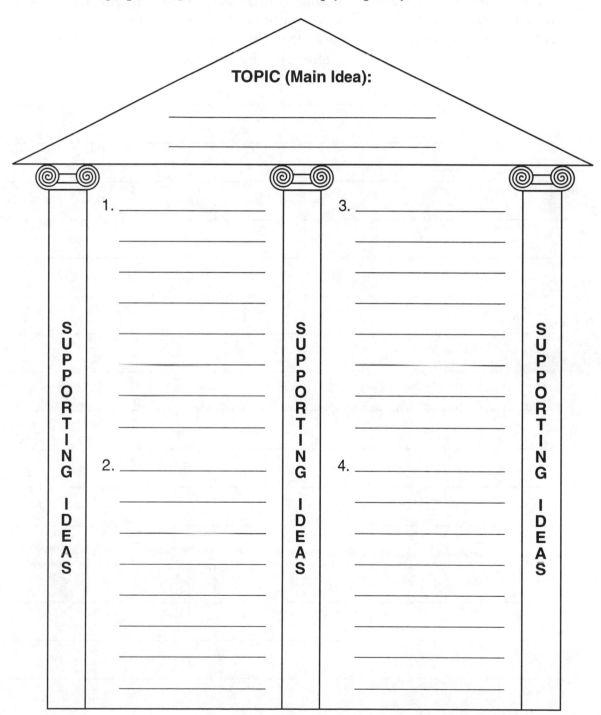

Writing Assignment
Supporting the Topic

Directions: Now use the ideas you wrote on page 43 to help you write a letter to your principal. Try to convince him or her to choose your idea for celebrating World Day. Remember to include two or three reasons that support your idea. Write your letter on the lines below.

_____

_____

_____

_____

_____

_____

_____

_____

_____

_____

_____

_____

_____

_____

_____

Revising and Editing

You've gathered your ideas. You've organized them. You've put them down on paper. Now you're done, right?

WRONG! The best writers don't stop there. After they've written what they wanted to say, they go back and **edit** their work. They want to make sure their writing is the best it can be.

Some writers work with people who help them with their writing. These people are called **editors.** Editors polish other people's writing and help them make it the best it can be.

Being Your Own Editor

You can learn to polish your own writing in much the same way an editor does. After you finish putting your ideas down on paper, go back to the beginning. Read what you have written. This time pretend that you are an editor instead of a writer. Pretend that you are reading the ideas for the very first time.

Below are some qualities you should look for when you edit.

The Editor's Checklist

✍ I do my best writing when:

❑ My writing stays focused on my topic.

❑ My writing uses details to support my topic.

❑ My writing is well-organized and complete. It has a beginning, a middle, and an end.

❑ I use different kinds of words in my writing. I do not use the same words over and over.

❑ I use different kinds of sentences in my writing.

❑ I choose words that make my meaning clear.

❑ I spell the words correctly.

❑ My handwriting is easy for others to read.

❑ My sentences and proper names begin with a capital letter.

❑ My sentences end with a period, an exclamation mark, or a question mark.

The Editor's Tools

In addition to checklists, editors have many tools to help them in their work. The symbols shown below are just some of the tools that editors use.

≡ Make a capital letter.
╱ Make a small letter.
⋞ Take something out.
∧ Put something in.

Example:

My First Day at Camp

At first i̲ thought that camp wasn't what it was cracked up to be. ̲everything was fine through supper and sing-along, but at bedtime, things began to get awful. I forgot my toothbrush, M̷y roommate had not yet arrived, and I wished I hadn't felt too old to bring my teddy bear, s̲nuggles. I was about as ~~sad~~ *gloomy* as a nine-year-old could be until the counselor and my roommate came in together. w̲e laughed for a long time, A̷nd I knew the rest of the week would be as good as i̲ had imagined. ~~Then I was happy.~~

The next few pages will give you more tips to help you as you edit.

Lesson 12

Capitalization

What if you read a paragraph that looked like this?

> *a person Does not choose his brotHers And Sisters. we are usually Stuck with What we get. thEy can Be great Fun, but they Also can be terRible Pests. my Little brotHer mikey can be Both. with mikey, You never knOW what you'Re Going to geT.*

You would probably think, *What's going on here?* If there were no rules for capitalization, writing could get pretty weird.

You may not think much about capitalization rules when you **start** writing. You can't forget them altogether, though. If your writing is capitalized in strange ways, it will be harder for others to read. And they might take longer to read it. They may not want to bother reading your writing at all.

So, when you are editing your writing, always check for capitalization. Below are a few rules to help you out.

Always capitalize . . .

1. the first word of each new sentence.

   Our baseball team is doing really well this year. We haven't lost any games by more than ten runs.

2. people's names.

   Nakisha Barnes   Zac Hanson   Pocahontas
   Joey Smith   Jackie Joyner-Kersee   my cousin Harold

3. titles that go with people's names.

   Prince William   Mr. Krystal   Dr. Jane Jones
   President Clinton   General Powell   Auntie Em

4. words you use in place of your family members' names.

   Mom   Grandfather
   Dad   Grandma

5. names of cities, states, countries, nationalities, and languages.

   Trenton   Zaire   Asian
   New Jersey   English   Dutch

6. days, months, and holidays. (Do NOT capitalize seasons.)

   Friday, February 14 is Valentine's Day. It is just one of many winter holidays.

7. brand names.

   Nike shoes   Super Nintendo video games
   Captain Crunch cereal   Pepsi

8. titles of books, movies, and songs. Do not capitalize words such as *of*, *and*, or *the* unless they are the first or last word of the title.

   Tales of a Fourth Grade Nothing   *The Wizard of Oz*
   The Hunchback of Notre Dame   "The Hokey Pokey"

9. the word "I."

   Today I wrote a story about myself. The main characters in my story are me, myself, and I.

Practice Activity

Capitalization

Directions: Proofread the sentences below. Put the editor's marks for capitalization (‗) below each letter that should be capitalized. Then rewrite each sentence, capitalizing where necessary. You may look back at the rules on page 48 for help.

1. have you read *the girl who cried monster* by r. l. stine?

_____

_____

2. my cousin joseph from kenya speaks two languages: swahili and english.

_____

_____

3. on monday, february 17, our country will celebrate president's day.

_____

_____

4. this saturday, sophia, kwame, and i are planning to watch the movie *toy story*.

_____

_____

5. at camp this summer, we learned many campfire songs, including "baby bumble bee."

_____

_____

6. last year, mom, dad, my sister kallie, and i all moved from kalamazoo, michigan, to edison, new jersey.

   _____

   _____

7. new jerseyans come from many different cultural backgrounds, including african, asian, european, middle eastern, and native american.

   _____

   _____

8. my brother nathaniel and i searched all day long on saturday for a present for mom and dad.

   _____

   _____

9. on her trip to washington, d.c., elena saw statues of president abraham lincoln and president thomas jefferson.

   _____

   _____

10. grandma and i like the same kind of cereal: kellogg's frosted mini-wheats.

   _____

   _____

Lesson 13

End Punctuation

*Sometimes you have a lot to say and you are so excited—like, wow!!!—
that you just have to get it all out so you just keep going not knowing when to
end your sentences and when to begin new ones and when you have said
everything you wanted to say—what was I saying again???—and then said a
little more and a little more until you are out of breath . . .*

And so is your reader!

End punctuation tells your reader when one idea stops and another idea begins.
It also gives your reader a chance to breathe. Deciding which mark of end
punctuation to use is quite easy.

1. Do you want to ask a question? If you do, be sure to put a question mark at
    the end.

    Have you seen that movie about tornadoes?

    Do you like to listen to music?

2. Wow! Writing can be exciting! For writing that is *really* exciting, use an
    exclamation mark. But don't overdo it. Save exclamation marks only for those
    times when you really need them.

    Yikes!

    Yea! We won!

    Look out below!

3. Use a period for all the rest. Put a period at the end of statements that don't
    ask a question or show great emotion.

    I am glad it is finally spring.

    Rashme just moved to the United States.

Practice Activity

End Punctuation

Directions: Proofread the sentences below. Place a period **(.)**, question mark **(?)**, or exclamation point **(!)** on the blank at the end of each sentence.

1. Swimming is my favorite summer pastime ___

2. Are you looking forward to the game today ___

3. Ouch ___

4. Doria is learning to be a gymnast ___

5. What is your favorite television show ___

6. I just read another book in the *American Girl* series ___

7. Watch out for that car ___

8. Who is your best friend ___

9. Go team ___

10. Did you do a project for the science fair ___

Lesson 14

Spelling

> *Does speling realy matter when I right? I mean, my story is exciting, the*
> *poeple in it are funnie, what more do I nead?*

Maybe spelling doesn't matter so much when you are first gathering your ideas.
You know what you mean to say. But will anyone else?

Your job as an editor is to make sure that the writing is easy for others to read.
This is a great time to check for spelling errors. Below are a few spelling rules to
help you out.

Suffixes

You can add word parts onto the ends of words to make new words. The
"add-ons" attached to the ends of words are called **suffixes.** For example:

enjoy + able = enjoy<u>able</u>

or "able to be enjoyed"

Below are some suffixes you probably already know:

–able	love + able = lovable
–ible	sense + ible = sensible
–ion	act + ion = action
–ly	sad + ly = sadly
–ment	excite + ment = excitement
–ness	happy + ness = happiness
–ing	come + ing = coming

Sometimes suffixes can cause spelling problems. The next few pages will remind
you of the rules for adding suffixes.

Changing *y* to *i*

If a **consonant** comes right before the *y* at the end of a word, change the *y* to an *i* before adding the suffix.

pretty + ness = prett<u>iness</u>

If a **vowel** comes right before the *y*, do NOT change the *y* to an *i*.

destroy + ed = destroy<u>ed</u>

For suffixes beginning with *i* (-*ing*, -*ion*, -*ible*), do NOT change the *y*.

carry + ing = carry<u>ing</u>

Practice Activity 1
Changing *y* to *i*

Directions: Attach suffixes to the words below.

1. ugly + ness = _____

2. worry + ing = _____

3. annoy + ed = _____

4. fluffy + ness = _____

5. cry + ing = _____

Have you tried the spelling log yet?

In the appendix of this workbook, you will find a spelling log. It will help you track your progress as you improve your spelling. Any time your teacher points out a misspelled word in your work, record the correct spelling in the log beginning on page 137.

Practice Activity 2
Changing *y* to *i*

Directions: Edit the following sentences by crossing out the misspelled word. Then write the correct spelling on the line above it.

_____

1. Marcus enjoys *studiing* the stars.

_____

2. The story was a *fancyful* tale of giants, dragons, and gnomes.

_____

3. The mountain climber *carryed* his gear for many miles.

_____

4. The movie was much more *enjoiable* than Janet had expected.

_____

5. The goldfish must feel some *lonelyness* all by itself in the bowl.

Silent e

If the suffix begins with a **vowel** (*-able, -ible, -ion, -ing*), drop the silent *e* at the end of the word before adding the suffix.

> move + able = mov<u>able</u>

If the suffix begins with a **consonant** (*-ly, -ment, -ness*), keep the silent *e*.

> like + ness = like<u>ness</u>

There are some exceptions to these rules, such as:

> true + ly = tru<u>ly</u>

> whole + ly = whol<u>ly</u>

Practice Activity 3
Silent e

Directions: Attach the suffixes to the following words.

1. imagine + able = _____

2. hope + ful = _____

3. dare + ing = _____

4. time + less = _____

5. believe + able = _____

Practice Activity 4
Silent e

Directions: Edit the following sentences by crossing out the misspelled word. Then write the correct spelling on the line above it.

1. Megan is *saveing* her money for a new game she wants to buy.

2. My grandmother just turned *ninty* years old.

3. Aunt Marge is *comeing* over for dinner.

4. Todd didn't like the *strangness* of the creepy old house.

5. Logan collects *valueable* old baseball cards.

Plurals

For most words, add *-s* to form the plural.

      apple + s = apple<u>s</u>

      cup + s = cup<u>s</u>

      car + s = car<u>s</u>

For words ending in *s*, *ss*, *ch*, or *x*, add *-es*.

      dress + es = dress<u>es</u>

      church + es = church<u>es</u>

      ax + es = ax<u>es</u>

For words ending in a consonant plus *y*, change the *y* to *i* and add *-es*.

      fairy + es ⟶ fair✗ + i + es ⟶ fairies
      kitty + es ⟶ kitt✗ + i + es ⟶ kitties

 ## Practice Activity 5
Plurals

Directions: Make the following words into plurals.

	singular	plural
Example:	chair	chairs

    1. book   _____

    2. lady   _____

    3. glass   _____

    4. puppy   _____

    5. lunch   _____

Practice Activity 6

Plurals

Directions: Edit the following sentences by crossing out the misspelled word. Then write the correct spelling on the line above it.

_____

1. If you find a genie in a bottle, will it really give you three *wishs?*

_____

2. Monique got a new pack of *penciles* just before school started.

_____

3. Shelia's mom has a job taking care of *babys* in a daycare center.

_____

4. Jerry likes to visit the *monkies* in the zoo.

_____

5. When we moved, we packed up everything and put it all into *boxs*.

i and e Rules

i before *e*	except after *c*	or when saying "*ay*"
belief	ceiling	neighbor
niece	receive	weigh

I before *e*, except after *c* or when saying "*ay*" as in neighbor and weigh.

 Practice Activity 7

i and e Rules

Directions: Circle the word in parentheses ( ) that is spelled correctly.

1. Pocahontas was the daughter of a Native American (cheif, chief).

2. Mariah used her coat as a (shield, sheild) against the wind.

3. Queen Elizabeth II of England has (reigned, riegned) since 1952.

4. How many (freinds, friends) are you inviting to the party?

5. Before there were cars, some people traveled by (sleigh, sliegh) in the winter.

Look Out for Homonyms

Homonyms are words that sound alike but are spelled differently and mean different things. Below are a few of these tricky words to watch for.

aunt	My **Aunt** Flo suddenly screamed.
ant	She saw an **ant** in her bedroom.
by	The weather is fairly warm **by** June.
bye	Say good-**bye** to snowy weather.
buy	Let's rush out to **buy** swimsuits for the summer.
dear	Jennifer's pets are very **dear** to her.
deer	Her favorite is a pet **deer** named Bambi.
hear	Did you **hear** the news?
here	A dangerous storm will soon be **here.**
it's (it is)	**It's** time to feed our pet snake.
its	Last week the snake shed **its** skin.
meet	Would you like to **meet** Mr. Venison?
meat	He is the owner of the **meat** market.
write	Jamie's little sister is learning to **write** in cursive.
right	She is learning to slant her letters to the **right.**
road	Did Dorothy walk down the yellow brick **road?**
rode	I don't think that she **rode** her bike.
their	Cindy and Juan left **their** skates outside.
they're (they are)	**They're** inside getting a glass of lemonade.
there	The skates are still **there** by the front step.
threw	Shelly **threw** the ball.
through	It went **through** her mother's new stained-glass window.

to	Are you going **to** the state spelling bee?
two	**Two** students from our school will compete.
too	They think they'll win first place, **too.**

whose	**Whose** purple polka-dotted hat is this?
who's (who is)	**Who's** going to search for the owner?

where	**Where** are you going?
wear	You can't **wear** a swim suit to the shopping mall!

would	**Would** you please help Marcus?
wood	He is chopping some **wood** for the campfire.

Practice Activity 8

Homonyms

Directions: Circle the word in parentheses ( ) that best fits each sentence.

1. Scientists learn about animals that lived long ago (by, bye, buy) studying fossils.

2. If Margaret could (meat, meet) anyone from the past, she would choose Eleanor Roosevelt.

3. How long does it take a space shuttle (to, too, two) circle the earth?

4. If you were a girl living in the nineteenth century, you might (where, wear) long, heavy dresses.

5. Michael (through, threw) the basketball out of bounds.

6. Maybe one day you will grow up to (write, right) exciting stories like *The Hardy Boys* mysteries.

7. More than 200,000 people traveled to Washington, D.C., in 1963 to (hear, here) Martin Luther King, Jr.'s "I Have a Dream" speech.

8. Orville and Wilbur Wright successfully flew (there, their, they're) airplane for the first time in 1903.

9. The peacock is best known for the beauty of (its, it's) feathers.

10. Do you know (who's, whose) going to be in the school talent show this year?

 ## Practice Activity 9
Homonyms

Directions: This exercise will review other homonyms you should know. For each of the following words, write a sentence that uses the word correctly. You may use a dictionary to look up any words you are unsure of.

1. ate _____

   eight _____

2. blue _____

   blew _____

3. cent _____

   sent _____

4. close _____

   clothes _____

5. dew _____

   do _____

   due _____

6. fair _____

   fare _____

7. pair _____

   pear _____

8. hole _____

   whole _____

9. knew _____

   new _____

10. plain _____

    plane _____

11. son _____

    sun _____

12. steal _____

    steel _____

13. tail _____

    tale _____

14. weak _____

    week _____

15. you're _____

    your _____

Lesson 15

The Final Draft

As you read through your writing using the Editor's Checklist, you may decide to make changes in your work. The best writers often make changes as they work. Some writers make many changes. Others may make only a few. It is okay to erase or cross out as long as your changes are done neatly.

Your readers won't know whether they like your writing if they are unable to read it. Your final copy should be neat enough for others to read easily. You may want to write in cursive or you may want to print. Either is okay. If you have time, you may want to make a new copy of what you have written.

A basketball game is colorful, *noisy* loud, and exciting. When a person walks into the gym, she is surrounded with sights, *sounds,* and smells from all directions. everyone is *eager* excited for the game to begin.

A basketball game is colorful, noisy, and exciting. When a person walks into the gym, she is surrounded with sights, sounds, and smells from all directions. Everyone is eager for the game to begin.

Practice Activity

The Final Draft

Directions: Choose something you wrote for a previous lesson in this book. Revise your writing using the Editor's Checklist on page 46. Then rewrite your work neatly on the lines below.

_____

_____

_____

_____

_____

_____

_____

_____

_____

_____

_____

_____

_____

Sharing and Publishing

You've learned the basics of writing. You've read about the importance of revising and editing. And you've practiced various types of writing. Now it's time to share your writing with someone else. After all, this is the real enjoyment of writing.

You can share your writing in several ways. You can simply read it to a teacher, family member, or friend. Or you can give your writing to them to read for themselves. You can even publish your writing for many people to read.

So, what are we waiting for? Get ready to show the world what a great writer you have become!

Lesson 16

Sharing Your Writing

Writers share their work in many ways and for many reasons. A writer may simply want to entertain the reader. Or he or she may want to get ideas from the reader about how to improve the writing. Following are a few ideas for sharing your writing.

One way that writers share their work is to participate in a **reading.** At a reading, a writer reads from something he or she has written. Then the audience responds to what they have heard.

Practice Activity 1

An Author's Reading

Directions: Choose something you have written for a previous lesson in this book or for another school assignment. This should be a piece you would like to share with members of your class.

Read your writing aloud to your classmates. Listen carefully to any questions they may ask. Your audience might give you new ideas for adding to or revising your writing. Write any ideas you get from your audience on the page containing the writing, or you may use the lines below.

_____

_____

_____

_____

_____

Another way to share your writing is to participate in a **writers' workshop.** In a writers' workshop, the author gives a copy of his or her writing to another author. That person then tells what he or she likes about the writing. He or she also gives ideas for making the writing even better.

Practice Activity 2

The Writers' Workshop

Directions: Choose something you have written for a previous lesson in this book or for another school assignment. This should be a piece you would like to learn how to improve. Trade your writing with a partner.

Read your partner's writing carefully. On the lines below, write what you would like to tell your partner about his or her writing.

1. First tell your partner what you liked about the writing.

_____

_____

_____

_____

_____

2. Now give your partner ideas for making the writing even better.

_____

_____

_____

_____

You may wish to share your writing for many other reasons: to entertain someone, to inform them of important facts, to convince them of your ideas, and so on. Whatever the reason, pass it on!

Practice Activity 3

Pass It On!

Directions: Choose something you have written for a previous lesson in this book or for another school assignment. This should be a piece of writing you would like to share. Then answer the following questions about the writing.

1. What kind of writing is it? (Circle one.)

   • a story   • a report   • a poem

   • another type of writing: _____

2. What is it about?

   _____

   _____

3. Why do you want to share this writing? (Circle one.)

   • to entertain someone   • to inform someone

   • to persuade someone   • another reason: _____

4. Think about who might like to read your writing. For example, imagine that you have written a story about a time you went fishing and something exciting happened. In this case, you might like to share your writing with someone who enjoys reading about outdoor adventures.

   Look at the answers you wrote to questions 1–3. Who might enjoy reading the type of writing you have chosen? List as many people as you wish.

   _____   _____

   _____   _____

   _____   _____

Now share your writing with one or more of the people on your list. It's that easy!

Lesson 17

Publishing Your Writing

You may simply want to share your story, report, or poem with friends and family. Or you might want your writing to be read by many more pairs of eyes. Perhaps you want to have a report published in the school newspaper. You might want to write a letter to the editor of your local newspaper telling about things kids are doing in your school. You might even submit a story or poem to a magazine that publishes children's writing. These are just a few ways to have your work read by others.

Publishing Your Own Writing

When sharing your writing with friends and family, you might want to make it look special. This is the fun of publishing your writing yourself. Just follow these five steps:

Step 1: **Make a cover page.** When you have finished your writing, create a cover page that has the title and your name. Type or print this neatly. Use heavier paper for the cover page. You also can use colored paper or artwork to make it more attractive.

Step 2: **Type or write neatly on one side of each page.** Be sure to revise and edit your writing. Then copy the final version on clean paper. Be sure that your handwriting is easy to read.

Step 3: **Add artwork to help tell the story.** Adding artwork to your writing will make it more fun to read. You can use drawings, photos, or even a collage.

Step 4: **Add a back page.** Add a blank piece of paper at the end. The paper should be the same as is used for the front cover.

Step 5: **Attach all the pages.** Now you're ready to attach everything. An easy way is to staple the pages together along one side. Place a staple at the top, middle, and bottom. Your "publication" is now finished.

Practice Activity 1
Publishing Your Own Writing

Directions: Choose something you have written, either in this book or for another school assignment. This should be a piece of writing you would like to share. Following the five steps listed on page 71, "self-publish" the piece of writing you chose.

Getting Your Writing Published

Another way to share your writing is to have it published by a magazine or newspaper.

Step 1:   **Select a publication.** Go to the local library or bookstore. Find newspapers or magazines that have articles similar to what you have written or would like to write. How long are the articles? Are the publications read by kids your age? Or are they read by adults?

Now read some of the articles. Is your writing similar? Are the articles on similar topics? Does the publication have stories or poems? Will your writing appeal to the readers of the magazine or newspaper?

Practice Activity 2

Selecting a Publication

Directions: Choose something you have written, either in this book or for another school assignment. This should be a piece of writing you would like to share.

Next, visit a library or bookstore. Look at several publications. Choose one that you think is most likely to publish the writing you chose. Once you have done this, answer the following questions.

1. What is the name of the publication?

   _____

2. What is the mailing address?

   _____

   _____

3. What is the editor's name? (His or her name will be listed on a page in the front part of the publication.)

   _____

Step 2: **Send for the Writer's Guidelines.** Before you send your writing to a magazine, you should first obtain a copy of the **writer's guidelines.** The writer's guidelines will tell you many things about the publication, such as:

- the types of stories or articles it publishes
- the number of words the story or article should have
- where to send the story or article
- any special instructions writers need to follow

Look at the letter below.

Ms. Judith Wordstar
Editor
KidsFirst Magazine
7654 3rd Street
Big City, USA 01234

Dear Ms. Wordstar:

I am requesting a copy of the writer's guidelines for *KidsFirst Magazine*. I have included a self-addressed, stamped envelope for your convenience.

Thank you for your help.

Sincerely,

David Wilson

David Wilson

Once you read the writer's guidelines, you will know more about the publication. This will give you a better chance of being published.

Practice Activity 3

The Writer's Guidelines

Directions: Write a letter to the editor whose name and address you wrote on page 73. (Always use the person's name. Never send something to "The Editor.") This letter should request the writer's guidelines simply and clearly. You may use the lines below to plan your letter.

_____

_____

_____

_____

_____

_____

_____

_____

_____

_____

_____

_____

Make sure to include a stamped envelope with your address written on the front. Editors will not pay for envelopes or postage.

Step 3:   **Submit Your Writing.** If you decide to submit your writing, it is important to include a letter that explains what the article or story is about. Here is an example:

Mr. Michael Goodwriter
Editor
Travelwise Magazine
5555 5th Avenue
Somewhere, USA 09876

Dear Mr. Goodwriter:

I am sending you a 300-word article about a new summer travel program for children from rural schools. The program pays all expenses for these children to visit Washington, D.C.

This article would be perfect for the Kids' Travel section of *Travelwise Magazine*. Many families will find this program to be a great way for their children to visit our nation's capital.

Please return the article in the enclosed self-addressed, stamped envelope.

Sincerely,

Tina Jackson

Tina Jackson

Practice Activity 4

Submitting Your Writing

Directions: Following the writer's guidelines you received from the publisher, submit your writing. Be sure to include a letter that tells about your writing. You can use the lines below to plan your letter.

_____

_____

_____

_____

_____

_____

_____

_____

_____

_____

_____

_____

_____

_____

_____

_____

To make sure you've done your best, complete the checklist on page 78 before submitting your work.

The Editor's Checklist

✍   I have my best chance of being published when:

❏   I have read a copy of the publication to learn more about it.

❏   I have written to the editor for a copy of the writer's guidelines.

❏   My writing follows the writer's guidelines and appeals to the readers of the magazine or newspaper.

❏   I have written a letter to the editor to send with my article or story. The letter has a greeting, a body, and a closing.

❏   My writing is well-organized and complete.

❏   My writing stays focused on my topic.

❏   I have carefully revised and edited my writing.

❏   I have typed my writing, or my handwriting is easy for others to read.

❏   All the words are spelled correctly.

❏   The copy of my writing is neat and clean.

Practice Topics

This section of the workbook will give you practice in several different kinds of writing. Ten activities will guide you through the writing process. As you work through these activities, you will write:

- a response to reading
- a response to viewing
- a fictional narrative (a story you make up)
- a personal experience narrative (a story about you)
- a poem
- an informational report
- a personal letter
- a persuasive piece
- a set of directions
- a journal entry

Response to Reading

You can get ideas for your writing from stories or poems. When you read a story, you might imagine yourself as one of the characters. Or you might imagine a different ending for the story. Sometimes stories and poems will remind you of events in your own life that you want to tell about. Reading can even give you ideas for a made-up story of your own.

Read the following story. You will use it later to help you gather ideas for writing.

The Tent
by Lance Ryder

Brenda, Carlotta, and I were going camping with twelve other girls. We wanted to be the first to get our tent set up. All week long, we practiced in Carlotta's backyard.

The night before the trip, Brenda said, "Let's just practice five more times." Each time, we were a little bit faster. By the fifth time, we were all sure we would be first. We stayed overnight at Carlotta's because we were leaving early in the morning.

At 7:00, my grandmother came to pick us up in her van. "Good morning," *mi abuelita** said. "You girls hop in and I'll take you to the campground."

On the way, we talked about how much fun it would be to be the first to set up our tent. Carlotta said, "After we get our tent set up, let's go around and help everyone else put up theirs."

When we got to the campground, our leader and the other campers were also arriving. Abuelita said, "Why don't two of you help unload the van. The other one can go select a spot for your tent."

I found a great spot close to the lake. Then I ran back to the van to get Brenda and Carlotta.

When I got there, the other girls were staring open-mouthed at the

---

* *mi abuelita* means "my grandmother" in Spanish.

pile of sleeping bags. I could see that Abuelita was trying hard not to smile.

"Come on, you two," I said. "Grab the tent and let's go."

Carlotta and Brenda both looked at me. "But Carmen, we forgot the tent!" Carlotta said. "It's still standing in my backyard!"

Prewriting Activity
Response to Reading

Directions: For this exercise, you will answer questions that will help you think about the story you just read. Later you will use this page to help you write about the story.

1. How do the girls in the story prepare for their camping trip?

    _____

2. What happens when the girls arrive at their campsite?

    _____

3. How do you think the girls feel at the end of the story? Why?

    _____

    _____

4. Think about a time when you planned carefully but something went wrong. What happened?

    _____

    _____

    _____

5. How did you feel?

    _____

    _____

    _____

Writing Assignment
Response to Reading

Directions: For this exercise, you will write a response to the story "The Tent." You will tell about a time when you planned carefully but something went wrong.

The writing you do for this exercise will be scored. Look at the box below. The checklist shows how you can earn your best score.

The Editor's Checklist

✎ I will earn my best score if:

❑ My writing tells about a time when I planned carefully but something went wrong.

❑ My writing tells about how I planned.

❑ My writing tells what went wrong and how I felt.

❑ My writing tells how my experience was similar to or different from the story.

❑ My writing tells many details about my experience.

❑ My writing has a beginning, a middle, and an end.

❑ I use different kinds of words in my writing. I do not use the same words over and over.

❑ I spell the words correctly.

❑ My sentences and proper names begin with a capital letter.

❑ My sentences end with a period, an exclamation mark, or a question mark.

Write your response to reading on the next page of your workbook. Use a pencil to write your response. You may make any editing changes in your work. If you need to change your writing, make sure you cross out or erase completely the writing you do not want to keep. Remember that writers often make changes as they work.

A Response to Reading — First Draft

_____

_____

_____

_____

_____

_____

_____

_____

_____

_____

_____

_____

_____

_____

_____

_____

_____

_____

When you have finished writing, use the checklist to revise and edit your work.

A Response to Reading — Final Draft

If you wish, recopy your work.

_____

_____

_____

_____

_____

_____

_____

_____

_____

_____

_____

_____

_____

_____

_____

_____

_____

_____

Response to Viewing

Things you see can give you ideas for writing. A television series about sharks, a photo of Yellowstone National Park, an unusual piece of artwork in a children's museum—all these might spark your imagination.

When writing about something you have seen or are seeing, ask yourself the following questions:

- What are you looking at?
- What details do you notice?
- What does the object remind you of?
- How do you feel when you look at the object?
- Can you tell a story (real or made-up) about the object?

Prewriting Activity

A Response to Viewing

Directions: Look at the picture below. It is a picture of a beach. For this exercise, you will answer questions to help you think about the picture. Later you will use this page to help you write about what you see.

1. What details do you notice in the picture?

_____

_____

2. What does the picture remind you of?

_____

_____

3. How do you feel when you look at the picture?

_____

_____

4. Can you tell a story (real or made-up) about the picture? If so, briefly describe the story you would tell.

_____

_____

_____

_____

_____

_____

Writing Assignment

A Response to Viewing

Directions: For this exercise, you will write about the picture of the beach. Your writing can be a real story, a made-up story, a poem, a report, or any other form you wish to use.

The writing you do for this exercise will be scored. Look at the box below. The checklist tells how you can earn your best score.

The Editor's Checklist

✍ I will earn my best score if:

❑ My writing tells something about the picture of the beach.

❑ My writing includes many details that support the main idea.

❑ My writing is well-organized with a beginning, a middle, and an end.

❑ I use words that make my meaning clear. I do not use the same words over and over.

❑ I spell the words correctly.

❑ My sentences and proper names begin with a capital letter.

❑ My sentences end with a period, an exclamation mark, or a question mark.

Write about the picture of the beach. Look back at the ideas you gathered on pages 85 and 86. You may use those ideas to help you write

On the next page of your workbook, write your response to viewing the picture of the beach. Use a pencil to write your response. You may make any editing changes in your work. If you need to change your writing, make sure to cross out or erase completely the writing you do not want to keep. Remember, writers often make changes as they work.

A Response to Viewing — First Draft

_____

_____

_____

_____

_____

_____

_____

_____

_____

_____

_____

_____

_____

_____

_____

_____

When you have finished writing, use the checklist to revise and edit your work.

A Response to Viewing — Final Draft

If you wish, recopy your work.

_____

_____

_____

_____

_____

_____

_____

_____

_____

_____

_____

_____

_____

_____

_____

_____

Fictional Narrative (A Story You Make Up)

A fictional narrative is a made-up story. Instead of being about real things, a fictional story is about things you imagine. There are three main things to think about when writing a story:

1. **Who is the story about?**

   The people in a story are called the *characters*.

2. **Where and when does the story take place?**

   This is called the *setting*.

3. **What happens in the story?**

   This is called the *plot*.

If you put all three of these together, you have a story. In a story, something happens **(plot)** to someone **(character),** somewhere **(setting).**

Let's look at each of these more closely.

1. **Characters**

   Who is the story about? Describe your characters. What do they look like? What do they act like? Is your story about a ten-year-old girl with long brown hair and a happy-go-lucky smile? Or is it about a jolly, wrinkly old man who walks with a cane? Animals or other creatures can also act as characters in your story.

   Readers like to hear characters speak for themselves. Instead of telling everything yourself, let the characters tell the story by talking to each other.

2. **Setting**

   Where does your story take place? In a jungle in Brazil? On the planet Belldaar? Or at the local shopping mall? Use details to describe your setting. Make your readers feel as if they are there. Use your five senses: What do things **look** like? If a character touches something, what does it **feel** like? What about **sounds, smells, tastes?**

   You may want to include details about the time of day or time of year. You can also make your story seem more real by adding details about the weather. Is it a snowy winter morning? Or is it a hot, steamy summer afternoon?

When does your story take place? Is it happening a hundred years ago when cowboys roamed the Wild West? Is it happening now, in the present? Or does your story take place a thousand years in the future?

3. Plot

In most stories, the plot has the main character get into some kind of trouble, and then get out again. Perhaps your character is captured by a spaceship on her way to school. Or maybe he is searching for a lost magic lamp and runs into dangers on the way. Your plot is limited only by your imagination.

 ## Prewriting Activity

Fictional Narrative

Directions: Have you ever had something happen that was completely unexpected? Have you ever planned to do something, then had everything go wrong? Have you ever begun an excuse with, "You'll never believe this . . ."?

For this activity, you will plan a made-up story. In your story, the main character must explain how he or she lost a library book. Your character's story can be realistic—something that really could happen. Or it can be a complete fantasy—a tale that is really far out! Remember, you are making up an excuse. It can be as wild and crazy as you want it to be.

The questions on the next page will help you plan your story. Write your ideas in the spaces provided. Remember, this prewriting work will not be scored.

Who is your story about? (Tell about the main character.)

What is the character's name?   How old is the character?

_____   _____

What is he or she like?_____

_____

Where and when does your story take place? (Tell about the setting.)

Where does the story take place?_____

_____

When does the story take place? (Past, present, or future? Time of year? Time of day?)

_____

What happens in your story? (Tell about the plot.)

What kind of trouble does the main character run into?_____

_____

_____

Why does this trouble cause the character to lose the library book?_____

_____

_____

What happens to get the character out of this trouble?_____

_____

_____

How does your story end?_____

_____

_____

_____

Writing Assignment

Fictional Narrative

Directions: For this exercise, you will write a fictional narrative (a made-up story). Your story will explain how the main character lost a library book. You may use the ideas you wrote on page 92 to help you write your story.

The writing you do for this exercise will be scored. Look at the box below. The checklist shows how you can earn your best score.

The Editor's Checklist

🖎 I will earn my best score if:

❏ My story gives the names of the characters.

❏ My story tells what kind of trouble the main character gets into.

❏ My story tells why this trouble causes the main character to lose a library book.

❏ My story tells how the main character gets out of this trouble.

❏ My story has a beginning, a middle, and an end.

❏ I use words that make my meaning clear. I do not use the same words over and over.

❏ I spell the words correctly.

❏ My sentences and proper names begin with a capital letter.

❏ My sentences end with a period, an exclamation mark, or a question mark.

Write your story on the next page of your workbook. Use a pencil to write your story. You may make any editing changes in your work. If you need to change your writing, make sure you cross out or erase completely the writing you do not want to keep. Remember that writers often make changes as they work.

Fictional Narrative (A Story You Make Up) — First Draft

_____

_____

_____

_____

_____

_____

_____

_____

_____

_____

_____

_____

_____

_____

_____

_____

When you have finished writing your story, use the checklist to revise and edit your work.

Fictional Narrative (A Story You Make Up) — Final Draft

If you wish, recopy your work.

_____

_____

_____

_____

_____

_____

_____

_____

_____

_____

_____

_____

_____

_____

_____

_____

_____

_____

_____

Personal Experience Narrative (A Story About You)

A personal experience narrative is a story you write about yourself. *You* are the main character. This kind of story describes something in your own life.

A personal experience narrative can be about all kinds of things. You might write about a time you visited a new place. Or you might write about a time you learned something new. The best things to write about are things that interest you—things that excite your imagination.

A personal experience narrative is a lot like other kinds of stories. It can include different kinds of people. It can be set in an interesting place. It can tell about something that happened to the people in the story. It has a beginning, a middle, and an end. It can be funny or serious.

Try to remember the details—how things looked, sounded, felt. Include whatever details you think will make your story seem more real to the reader. Don't worry about making yourself look good. Readers like writers who are honest about themselves.

Here are two examples of personal experience narratives. Which story do you like best?

Story #1

One day last summer, my grandmother and I went for a walk. We went to the Merry Dairy and had some ice cream. We talked for a while. She told me a story about my dad when he was a boy. The ice cream was good, and we had fun. I'm glad we went.

Story #2

One day last summer, my grandmother asked me if I would like to take a walk with her.

"Where to?" I asked.

"I thought we might go get some ice cream," she said.

I thought I would rather finish playing Super Nintendo. But, well, she *is* my grandmother. So I went.

We walked outside. It was a beautiful sunny day, even if it was a little hot. There was a nice breeze blowing. I couldn't help but think how pretty Grandma's silver hair looked in the sunlight.

The Merry Dairy is only a few blocks from my house, so it isn't a very long walk. We decided to take our time, though. While we walked, she told me a story about how my dad (he's her son) used to catch minnows to use as bait for fishing. He would keep them in jars underneath his bed until he was ready to use them. But by the time he was ready to go fishing, he would have already gotten attached to the minnows. He felt sorry for them and poured them back into the pond. "There wasn't a whole lot of fresh fish for dinner at our house in those days," she said.

We were glad when we rounded the corner and saw the Merry Dairy. The brief walk was warm enough to make an ice cream cone sound really good. I had chocolate chip cookie dough ice cream on a sugar cone. She had strawberry vanilla swirl. We ate every bite on our way back home.

Grandma lives in South Carolina. She comes to visit us here for a little while each summer. Since I don't get to see her very often, I especially enjoy the little bit of time I get to spend with her. I'm glad I picked ice cream over Super Nintendo that day. Spending time with her is super enough for me.

Which story do you think is more interesting? Why?

_____

_____

_____

Prewriting Activity

Personal Experience Narrative

Directions: Now you will plan a personal experience narrative of your own. Think back to a time you spent with someone special. It can be a time you spent with a family member or with your best friend. Or maybe you want to tell about a special time you spent with your pet.

Below are a few questions to help you plan your story. Remember, this prewriting work will not be scored.

1. Who did you spend this special time with?

_____

2. Where were you? _____

_____

3. What did you do? _____

_____

_____

_____

4. What was the weather like? _____

_____

5. What made the day special? _____

_____

_____

_____

6. What other details can you remember (sights, smells, sounds, tastes, feelings)?

_____

_____

_____

7. What else can you say about this time you spent with someone special?

_____

_____

_____

Writing Assignment

Personal Experience Narrative

Directions: Now you are going to write a personal story about a time you spent with someone special. You may use the ideas you wrote on pages 97 and 98 to help you write your story.

The writing you do for this exercise will be scored. Look at the box below. The checklist shows how you can earn your best score.

The Editor's Checklist

✍ I do my best writing when:

❑ My story tells about one time I spent with someone special.

❑ I tell the names of the people in my story.

❑ My story has many details about the special time.

❑ My story has a beginning, a middle, and an end.

❑ I use different kinds of words in my story. I do not use the same words over and over.

❑ I spell the words correctly.

❑ My sentences and proper names begin with a capital letter.

❑ My sentences end with a period, an exclamation mark, or a question mark.

Write your story on the next page of your workbook. Use a pencil to write your story. You may make any editing changes in your work. If you need to change your writing, make sure you cross out or erase completely the writing you do not want to keep. Remember that writers often make changes as they work.

Personal Experience Narrative
(A Story About You) — First Draft

_____

_____

_____

_____

_____

_____

_____

_____

_____

_____

_____

_____

_____

_____

_____

When you have finished writing your story, use the checklist to revise and edit your work.

Personal Experience Narrative (A Story About You) — Final Draft

If you wish, recopy your work.

_____

_____

_____

_____

_____

_____

_____

_____

_____

_____

_____

_____

_____

_____

_____

_____

_____

Poem

In Lesson 5, you learned how to use poetry to express your thoughts. Recall some of the special features of poetry:

- Poems often describe ordinary things in extraordinary ways.
- Poems often use "hard-working words" that appeal to the senses.
- Poems often use unusual comparisons. These comparisons might be in the form of similes, metaphors, or analogies.
- Poems make every word count. They say as much as possible in as few words as possible.
- Poems are written in lines and stanzas rather than in sentences and paragraphs.
- Some poems rhyme, but many do not.

Prewriting Activity

A Poem

Directions: For this activity, you will gather ideas for a poem. In your poem, you will describe something you see from where you are sitting in your classroom. The following questions will help you gather ideas for your poem.

1. From where you are sitting, look around the room. (You can also look out the window if you like, but do not leave your seat.) Locate an object in the room about which you would like to write. What object did you chose?

   _____

2. What does the object look like? Give as many details as you can.

   _____

   _____

   _____

   _____

3. What other special features does the object have? (For example: Does it have a smell? If you touched it, what would it feel like? Does it make sounds? Can it do other things?) Again, give as many details as you can.

_____

_____

_____

_____

4. What does the object remind you of? Try to make an unusual comparison. You can use a simile or a metaphor if you like. For example:

    The pencil sharpener chews pencils like a rabbit chews carrots.

_____

_____

_____

5. Is there anything else you would like to tell about the object?

_____

_____

_____

Writing Assignment

Poem

Directions: For this exercise, you will write a poem. Your poem will tell about an object you can see from where you are sitting in your classroom. You may use the ideas you wrote on pages 102 and 103 to help you write your poem.

The writing you do for this exercise will be scored. Look at the box below. The checklist tells how you can earn your best score.

The Editor's Checklist

✍ I will earn my best score if:

❑ My writing is in the form of a poem.

❑ My poem describes something ordinary in an extraordinary way.

❑ My poem uses lively words to describe things. My poem uses strong verbs.

❑ My poem uses comparisons (metaphors, similes, or analogies).

❑ My poem has no unnecessary words.

❑ I use words that make my meaning clear.

❑ I spell the words correctly.

Write your poem on the next page of your workbook. Use a pencil to write your poem. You may make any editing changes in your work. If you need to change your writing, make sure you cross out or erase completely the writing you do not want to keep. Remember, writers often make changes as they work.

Poem — First Draft

_____

_____

_____

_____

_____

_____

_____

_____

_____

_____

_____

_____

_____

_____

_____

_____

_____

When you have finished writing your poem, use the checklist to revise and edit your work.

Poem — Final Draft

If you wish, recopy your work.

_____

_____

_____

_____

_____

_____

_____

_____

_____

_____

_____

_____

_____

_____

_____

Informational Writing (A Report)

A report is a collection of information about a topic. It is written in paragraph form. It contains information that is true, not things that are made up.

Reports have many different uses. Reports can tell people about things that are important to them, such as the reports you read in newspapers or magazines. Reports can help people make decisions, such as reports that government leaders give to the President. Someone also might write a report as a way to learn more about a topic.

Writing a report is easy, and it can be lots of fun. Just follow these five steps:

Step 1: **Choose a topic.** Your teacher may assign a topic to you. Or you may choose a topic that is interesting to you. Pick something that makes you curious, something that you will enjoy learning more about.

Step 2: **Gather information.** Encyclopedias, newspapers, magazines, and books are all great sources of information. You may also want to interview someone who knows a lot about your topic. Ask your teacher or librarian for more ideas about gathering information.

Step 3: **Get organized!** Sort the information you have gathered.

- What is the main idea?

- What are the important ideas that support the main idea?

- What are the details that support each important idea?

Connect the supporting ideas and details in an organized way. Many reports are organized like this:

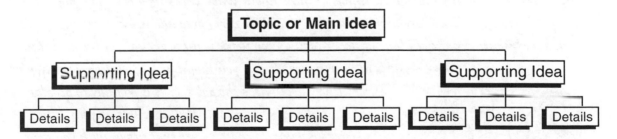

Step 4: **Put the information into paragraphs.** Use your own words. Don't copy someone else's words.

Step 5: **Write a summary or closing statement.** Write a sentence or two that summarizes what your report is all about.

Example

Anthony wants to earn a merit badge from the Campscout Club. One way he can earn a badge is to write an informational report. He has decided to write a report on how to choose a pet.

Anthony has gathered information from many sources. He has read about pets in the encyclopedia and in other books from the library. He has visited a pet store and talked to the people there. He has even talked to a veterinarian, a special kind of doctor just for pets. Here is how Anthony has decided to organize the information he has found:

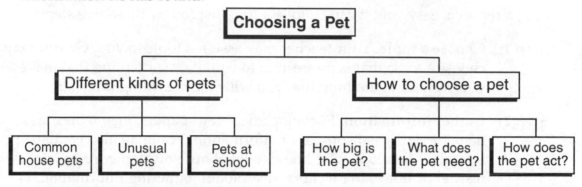

And here is Anthony's report:

There are all kinds of pets. Dogs, cats, birds, and fish are the most common pets that live in people's homes. Some pets are unusual. A Japanese child may have a mouse that she trains to dance to music. People who live in Antarctica may have penguins as pets. Sometimes schoolrooms will have pets, too. Girls and boys can take care of the pets and watch them grow. Hamsters, rabbits, snakes, and ants are pets sometimes found in schoolrooms.

There are many important things to think about when choosing a pet. How big is the pet? If it is very big, it will probably need a big place to live. A horse will not be very happy in a small apartment! What does the pet need? How much work is it to take care of the pet? If no one is at your house all day, you might pick a goldfish. They don't get very lonely. How does the pet act? Is it friendly to people? Will it need a lot of training? Will it gobble up your little sister? Be sure to choose a pet that fits in with you and your family.

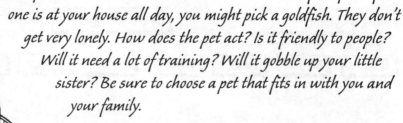

There are many different kinds of pets to choose from. There are also many things to think about when choosing a pet. Be careful to make a choice that is right for you and your future pet.

Prewriting Activity

Informational Writing

Directions: Now you will write a report on your own. The notes below and on the next page have been gathered from books on Antarctica. The notes are not in any particular order. Read through the notes once, marking the things that you find interesting. You might also want to locate Antarctica on a globe or map. Then use the questions on page 111 to help you plan your report.

from an encyclopedia article on Antarctica

Antarctica is the coldest region in the world, even colder than the North Pole.

Winter in Antarctica lasts from May until August.

It never rains in Antarctica, but it snows a little each year.

The temperature in Antarctica almost never gets above freezing.

Summer in Antarctica lasts from December until February.

from *The Icy Wild Kingdom*

Animals living in the waters around Antarctica include fish, penguins, seals, whales, and birds.

Not very many kinds of plants or insects can survive in the cold temperatures on Antarctica.

Millions of years ago—before Antarctica was covered with ice—trees, dinosaurs, and small animals lived there.

Penguins cannot fly.

The largest animal that lives on land in Antarctica is a type of fly that is only 1/2 inch long.

from *The Geography of Antarctica*

Antarctica is the continent that covers the South Pole.

Antarctica is buried in ice and snow.

Just like other continents, Antarctica has mountains, lowlands, and valleys.

Millions of years ago, Antarctica was not covered with ice.

Antarctica is surrounded by the Atlantic, Indian, and Pacific oceans.

If the ice on Antarctica melted, the water in all the oceans would rise.

Some of the valleys on Antarctica have lakes.

Many cities on the coasts of these oceans would be flooded if the oceans rose.

from *Research on Antarctica*

Today, over 30 research stations are located in Antarctica.

Researchers in Antarctica study things like earthquakes, gravity, and the solar system.

One research station, McMurdo Station, has about 1,000 people living there.

Some people believe that research on Antarctica can solve many mysteries about the earth's past.

Some scientists want to use Antarctica as a source for fresh water.

Most people doing research in Antarctica live there during the summer.

Large icebergs could be towed to places needing water, like deserts.

Very few people stay in Antarctica for the winter.

Researchers also study weather on Antarctica.

Directions: You will use the facts on pages 109 and 110 to write a brief report on Antarctica. (You do not need to use all the facts.) The questions below will help you organize your ideas. Remember, this prewriting work will not be scored.

1. What is the **topic** or **main idea** of your report?

_____

_____

What important ideas will support your topic or main idea?	List details that support the important ideas you have chosen.
Idea #1:	Details:
Idea #2:	Details:
Idea #3:	Details:

2. Write a closing statement that summarizes the most important ideas in your report.

_____

Writing Assignment

Informational Writing

Directions: For this exercise, you will write a report on Antarctica. Your report may be from one to several paragraphs long. You may use the information you wrote on page 111 to help you write your report.

The writing you do for this exercise will be scored. Look at the box below. The checklist shows how you can earn your best score.

The Editor's Checklist

✍ I do my best writing when:

❑ My report gives a main idea.

❑ My report gives important ideas that support the main idea.

❑ My report gives details to support each of the important ideas.

❑ My report has a closing statement that summarizes the main idea and other important ideas.

❑ My report is complete.

❑ I use words that make my meaning clear. I do not use the same words over and over.

❑ I spell the words correctly.

❑ My sentences and proper names begin with a capital letter.

❑ My sentences end with a period, an exclamation mark, or a question mark.

Write your report on the next page of your workbook. Use a pencil to write your report. You may make any editing changes in your work. If you need to change your writing, make sure you cross out or erase completely the writing you do not want to keep. Remember, writers often make changes as they work.

Informational Writing (A Report) — First Draft

_____

_____

_____

_____

_____

_____

_____

_____

_____

_____

_____

_____

_____

_____

_____

When you have finished writing your report, use the checklist to revise and edit your work.

Informational Writing (A Report) — Final Draft

If you wish, recopy your work.

_____

_____

_____

_____

_____

_____

_____

_____

_____

_____

_____

_____

_____

_____

_____

Letter

The main things that you need in a letter are a **greeting**, a **body**, and a **closing**. Look at the letter below.

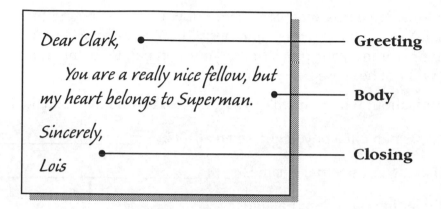

Greeting

Begin your letter by greeting the person you are writing. Some sample greetings are:

- Dear Marsha,
- Dear Aunt Claire,
- Dear Mr. Jordan,

Body

The body of a letter tells the reader what you want to say. It can be as long as you want it to be. It should be written in paragraph form. The body of a letter should do the following:

- be complete
- use words that make your meaning clear
- use words that are spelled correctly
- begin sentences and proper names with a capital letter
- end sentences with a period, an exclamation mark, or a question mark

Closing

The closing says a final good-bye to the reader and lets him or her know who wrote the letter. Sample closings are shown below.

Sincerely,   Yours truly,   Love,

Chelsea Clinton   Grandpa Wilson   Billy Bob

Prewriting Activity

Letter

Directions: Now you will plan a letter of your own. Pretend that you have a pen pal. Your pen pal lives in another state. You have never met him or her. You are planning your first letter to your pen pal. Remember, this prewriting work will not be scored.

1. Think about who you will be writing to. (You'll have to make this part up.)

   Is your pen pal a boy, a girl, or an adult? _____

   What is your pen pal's name? _____

   Where does your pen pal live? _____

2. To start your letter you will need a **greeting.** What will you say in your greeting?

   _____

3. Now you will plan the **body** of your letter. Your pen pal will want to learn about you. What are some things you would like to say about yourself? You could write about where you live, what your family is like, or what your school is like. Or you could tell your pen pal about your friends or about the kinds of things you like to do. Write at least three ideas on the lines below:

   _____

   _____

   _____

   Are there any questions you would like to ask your pen pal? If so, what are they?

   _____

   _____

   _____

4. You're almost finished planning your letter. What would you like to say in your **closing?**

   _____

   _____

Writing Assignment

Letter

Directions: For this exercise, you will write a letter. Pretend you are writing to a pen pal who lives in another state. You have never met your pen pal. This is the first letter you have written to him or her. You may use the information you wrote on page 116 to help you write your letter.

The writing you do for this exercise will be scored. Look at the box below. The checklist shows how you can earn your best score.

The Editor's Checklist

✍ I do my best writing when:

❑ I use the form for a letter with a greeting, a body, and a closing.

❑ My letter greets my pen pal with his or her name.

❑ My letter tells my pen pal who I am and tells something about me.

❑ The body of my letter is complete. It has a beginning, a middle, and an end.

❑ I use words that make my meaning clear. I do not use the same words over and over.

❑ I spell the words correctly.

❑ My sentences and proper names begin with a capital letter.

❑ My sentences end with a period, an exclamation mark, or a question mark.

Write your letter on the next page of your workbook. Use a pencil to write your letter. You may make any editing changes in your work. If you need to change your writing, make sure you cross out or erase completely the writing you do not want to keep. Remember, writers often make changes as they work.

Letter — First Draft

_____

_____

_____

_____

_____

_____

_____

_____

_____

_____

_____

_____

_____

_____

_____

_____

When you have finished writing your letter, use the checklist to revise and edit your work.

Letter — Final Draft

If you wish, recopy your work.

_____

_____

_____

_____

_____

_____

_____

_____

_____

_____

_____

_____

_____

_____

_____

Persuasive Writing

Sometimes you might want to write to convince others of your ideas. One way to do this is to write a letter to the editor of your local newspaper. A letter to the editor of a newspaper gives an opinion. It tells the newspaper's readers what you think. It may also try to encourage them to think as you do.

There are many reasons for writing a letter to the editor. Here are some examples:

- to tell what you think about a law that will be voted on
- to support a political candidate
- to suggest ideas to improve the community
- to discuss an issue that is interesting to readers
- to thank a person, a group of people, or an organization for their service to the community

In other words, a letter to the editor can be about anything that is interesting to readers. It should be polite, but brief. It should also be direct and clearly state the reasons you are writing. Like other letters, a letter to the editor should have a greeting, a body, and a closing.

 ## Prewriting Activity

Persuasive Writing

Directions: Pretend that your school has just received money to buy something new for the students. School officials are trying to decide whether to spend the money on new books for the school library or on new exercise equipment for the playground. They are asking students for their opinions. You have decided to write a letter to the editor of your school paper. You want to convince school officials and other students to think the way you do.

The questions below will help you think of things to put in your letter. Remember that this prewriting work will not be scored.

1. What do you think the money should be spent on? Circle your answer below:

> books for the library

> exercise equipment for the playground

2. How would your choice help the students at your school? List as many reasons as you can.

_____

_____

_____

_____

3. Why do you think the other choice is not as important to the school as your choice?

_____

_____

_____

_____

4. What would you like other students to do as a result of reading your letter?

_____

_____

_____

_____

5. What would you like the school officials to do as a result of reading your letter?

_____

_____

_____

_____

Writing Assignment

Letter to the Editor

Directions: For this exercise, you will write a letter to the editor of the school paper.

In your letter you will state your opinion about what should be purchased for your school: new books or new exercise equipment. Give several reasons to support your opinion. Tell your readers what you would like them to do as a result of reading your letter. You may use the information you wrote on pages 120 and 121 to help you write your letter.

The writing you do for this exercise will be scored. Look at the box below. The checklist shows how you can earn your best score.

The Editor's Checklist

✍ I do my best writing when:

❑ My letter tells what I think should be bought for the school: books or exercise equipment.

❑ My letter gives several reasons to support my opinion.

❑ My letter tells the readers what I would like them to do as a result of reading my letter.

❑ I use the form for a letter with a greeting, a body, and a closing.

❑ I use words that make my meaning clear. I do not use the same words over and over.

❑ I spell the words correctly.

❑ My sentences and proper names begin with a capital letter.

❑ My sentences end with a period, an exclamation mark, or a question mark.

Write your letter on the next page of your workbook. Use a pencil to write your letter. You may make any editing changes in your work. If you need to change your writing, make sure you cross out or erase completely the writing you do not want to keep. Remember, writers often make changes as they work.

Letter to the Editor — First Draft

_____

_____

_____

_____

_____

_____

_____

_____

_____

_____

_____

_____

_____

_____

_____

_____

_____

When you have finished writing your letter, use the checklist to revise and edit your work.

Letter to the Editor — Final Draft

If you wish, recopy your work.

_____

_____

_____

_____

_____

_____

_____

_____

_____

_____

_____

_____

_____

_____

_____

_____

_____

_____

Directions

Directions are very important. They may tell how to play a video game, how to put together a new bicycle, or how to do a homework assignment. Jobs like these are much simpler if the directions are clear and easy to understand.

To make directions clear, remember to:

- **List the major steps.**
- **Put the steps in order** from beginning to end.
- **Break down each major step** into smaller steps.
- **Read over the directions.** Try to imagine that you are reading them for the first time. Are they easy to understand? Have you left out anything? If possible, have someone else read your directions to see if they can follow them.
- **Revise your directions** if they don't seem clear enough.

Directions may be written in "step-by-step" form, such as the directions given below.

Seek-and-Go-Hide

This game is a lot like Hide-and-Go-Seek, but with a twist.

Step 1: Choose one person to be "It."

Step 2: The person who is "It" leaves the group to hide. The rest of the group stays back and counts to 100.

Step 3: After counting to 100, the group splits up and tries to find the person who is "It." As people in the group find the person who is "It," they hide along with him or her. Soon the number of people in hiding grows and grows.

Step 4: The last person to find the rest of the group is chosen to be "It" for the next round of "Seek-and-Go-Hide."

You may wish to decide on boundaries for the game before you start. You may want to limit the game to your backyard, one side of your street, or your entire block.

Directions may also be written in the form of a paragraph. Whichever way you write them, they must be clear, easy to understand, and not leave out anything important.

Prewriting Activity

Directions

Directions: Your class is publishing a book called *The Best Games Ever*. Your teacher has asked you to write directions for your favorite game. Pretend that no one in your class has ever played the game before. You need to write directions that are clear and complete.

(TIP: Try not to pick a game that is hard to explain. Simple games are easier to describe to other people.)

Picture in your mind how your game begins. The questions on the next page will help you think about each step of your game. Write your ideas in the spaces provided. Remember, this prewriting work will not be scored.

To Plan Your Game

BEGIN HERE

Where is the game played?

How many people are needed to play the game?

ONE WAY

What objects do you need to play the game?

What needs to be decided before the game starts?

How does the game begin?

ONE WAY

What happens next?

How does the game end?

Is there a winner? If so, how is the winner chosen?

START

STOP

Writing Assignment

Directions

Directions: For this exercise, you will write complete directions telling how to play your favorite game. You will write your directions in paragraph form.

Your directions need to be organized and clear. They should tell everything a person needs to know to learn how to play the game. Imagine that the person reading your directions has never played the game before. You may use the ideas you wrote on page 127 to help you write your directions.

The writing you do for this exercise will be scored. Look at the box below. The checklist shows how you can earn your best score.

The Editor's Checklist

✍ I do my best writing when:

❑ My directions are in the form of a paragraph.

❑ My directions have all the major steps for playing the game.

❑ My directions put the steps in order from beginning to end.

❑ My directions break down each major step into smaller steps when necessary.

❑ My directions are well organized and complete.

❑ I use words that make my meaning clear. I do not use the same words over and over.

❑ I spell the words correctly.

❑ My sentences and proper names begin with a capital letter.

❑ My sentences end with a period, an exclamation mark, or a question mark.

Write your directions on the next page of your workbook. Use a pencil to write your directions. You may make any editing changes in your work. If you need to change your writing, make sure you cross out or erase completely the writing you do not want to keep. Remember, writers often make changes as they work.

Directions — First Draft

_____

_____

_____

_____

_____

_____

_____

_____

_____

_____

_____

_____

_____

_____

_____

_____

_____

_____

When you have finished writing your directions, use the checklist to revise and edit your work.

Directions — Final Draft

If you wish, recopy your work.

_____

_____

_____

_____

_____

_____

_____

_____

_____

_____

_____

_____

_____

_____

_____

_____

Journal

A journal is a record of your life. It can tell about things that happened in a day, a month, or a whole year. It can tell as much or as little as you want it to. It's about you—your feelings, what you've learned, or experiences you've had.

Some types of journals are described below.

- A **diary** contains descriptions of things that happen each day. A diary can include your thoughts about the things happening in your life.

- A **travel log** is a description of a journey you've taken. A travel log might include how you got there, what you saw, and how you felt.

- A **learning log** is where you describe things you learn as you read, work, or study. A learning log is sometimes shared with a teacher.

Journal entries can be written as a letter or in paragraph form. Most journal entries include the date they were written. A journal should be well written and understandable when you go back to read it later. Include details that will make your journal interesting. Make it come alive to your reader—even if the only person to ever read it is you.

Prewriting Activity

Journal

Directions: Last summer, Gracie went on vacation with her family to New Orleans, Louisiana. While they were there, Gracie kept a travel log. In her travel log, she wrote about what she and her family did each day.

June 6, 1997

Today we visited the Aquarium of the Americas in New Orleans. One part of the aquarium is a tank in the shape of a tunnel that people can walk through. When you are inside the tunnel, fish and other wildlife are all around you. It's almost like you are underwater with them.

There were many different kinds of fish at the aquarium—I doubt anyone could count them all! They came in all shapes and sizes: round and flat, big and little, long and short. They also were many different colors and patterns: red, green, blue, striped, and polka dotted. Seeing all the different kinds of fish made me think about how people are different from each other, too. If we were all alike, we wouldn't be very interesting, would we?

Today was fun. I wonder where we will go tomorrow?

The journal entry you just read tells about a real day in the writer's life. For your next activity, think about a real day in your life. It should be a day that you want to share with your classmates and your teacher.

The questions below and on the following page will help you write about a real day in your life. For each question, write down as many ideas as you can think of. Don't judge your ideas yet. Just write them as fast as you can. Your ideas should be things you would like to share with your classmates. Remember, this prewriting work will not be scored.

1. What are some real days that you might like to write about?

    _____

    _____

    _____

    _____

    _____

2. Which idea do you like best? Circle it in your list above.

Now, think about the details of the day you want to write about.

3. What happened? _____

    _____

    _____

    _____

    _____

4. When did it happen? _____

    _____

5. Where did it happen? _____

   _____

6. How old were you? _____

7. Who else was there? _____

   _____

   _____

Think about the following things related to the experiences you are writing about. Read each word, then close your eyes and remember that part of your experience. Reliving the day might help you decide what to include in your journal entry.

     Sights   Sounds   Smells   Feelings   Thoughts

8. Is there anything else about the day that you would like to tell?

   _____

   _____

   _____

   _____

Writing Assignment

Journal

Directions: For this exercise, you will write a journal entry. In your journal entry, you will tell about a real day in your own life. Tell about something you would like to share with your teachers and your classmates.

Use as many details as you can remember about the day. Be sure to include the date and the location of the event. (If you can't remember the date, you can make this part up.) You may use the ideas you wrote on pages 132 and 133 to help you write your entry.

The writing you do for this exercise will be scored. Look at the box below. The checklist shows how you can earn your best score.

The Editor's Checklist

✍ I do my best writing when:

❏   My journal entry describes a day in my life.

❏   My journal entry has a date on it.

❏   My journal entry tells where the events I am describing took place.

❏   My journal entry uses details to describe things.

❏   I use words that make my meaning clear. I do not use the same words over and over.

❏   I spell the words correctly.

❏   My sentences and proper names begin with a capital letter.

❏   My sentences end with a period, an exclamation mark, or a question mark.

Write your journal entry on the next two pages of your workbook. Use a pencil to write your journal entry. You may make any editing changes in your work. If you need to change your writing, make sure you cross out or erase completely the writing you do not want to keep. Remember, writers often make changes as they work.

Journal Entry — First Draft

_____

_____

_____

_____

_____

_____

_____

_____

_____

_____

_____

_____

_____

_____

_____

_____

_____

When you have finished writing your journal entry, use the checklist to revise and edit your work.

Journal Entry — Final Draft

If you wish, recopy your work.

_____

_____

_____

_____

_____

_____

_____

_____

_____

_____

_____

_____

_____

_____

_____

_____

_____

Spelling Log

Keeping a spelling log will help you improve your spelling. Most of us are not terrible spellers. We just misspell the same words over and over.

Any time your teacher points out a misspelled word in your work, record the correct spelling in your log. Then spell the word correctly four times. This will help you remember how to spell the word right the next time.

Correct Spelling _____

_____ _____

_____ _____

Correct Spelling _____

_____ _____

_____ _____

Correct Spelling _____

_____ _____

_____ _____

Correct Spelling _____

_____ _____

_____ _____

Correct Spelling _____

_____ _____

_____ _____

Correct Spelling _____

_____ _____

_____ _____

Correct Spelling _____

_____ _____

_____ _____

Correct Spelling _____

_____ _____

_____ _____

Correct Spelling _____

_____   _____

_____   _____

Correct Spelling _____

_____   _____

_____   _____

Correct Spelling _____

_____   _____

_____   _____

Correct Spelling _____

_____   _____

_____   _____

Correct Spelling _____

_____   _____

_____   _____

Correct Spelling _____

_____   _____

_____   _____

Correct Spelling _____

_____   _____

_____   _____

Correct Spelling _____

_____   _____

_____   _____

Correct Spelling _____

_____   _____

_____   _____

Correct Spelling _____

_____   _____

_____   _____

Correct Spelling _____

_____   _____

_____   _____

Correct Spelling _____

_____   _____

_____   _____

New Jersey Elementary School Proficiency Assessment (ESPA)

Grade 4 Writing Objectives

Students construct and extend meaning through writing.

A. A student should know:

- That writing is a way of thinking, learning, and communicating.
- That speaking, listening, reading, and viewing contribute to writing.
- Writing processes (e.g., prewriting, drafting, revising, editing, sharing, publishing).
- Strategies for composing different types of writing.
- Forms (e.g., stories, poetry, reports), elements (e.g., main idea, point of view, opening, closing), grammatical conventions, and literary devices (e.g., simile, metaphor, alliteration).
- Audiences and purposes for writing.
- That critical thinking, reflection, and analysis contribute to the experience of writing.
- That reflection on multiple perspectives and texts (written, oral, and visual) helps the writer construct meaning.

B. A student should be able to:

- Draw on experience to compose.
- Engage in the full process of writing (e.g., prewriting, drafting, revising, editing, sharing, publishing).
- Use and adjust composition strategies to write for different purposes.
- Select, use, and adjust types of writing, elements, grammatical conventions, and literary devices when composing.
- Evaluate his or her own writing using multiple sources.

New Jersey Language Arts and Literacy Standards and Progress Indicators

Standard 3.3: All students will write in clear, concise, organized language that varies in content and form for different audiences and purposes.

By the end of Grade 4, students:

1. Use speaking, listening, reading, and viewing to assist with writing.

2. Write from experiences, thoughts, and feelings.

3. Use writing to extend experience.

4. Write for a variety of purposes, such as to persuade, enjoy, entertain, learn, inform, record, respond to reading, and solve problems.

5. Write on self-selected topics in a variety of literary forms.

6. Write collaboratively and independently.

7. Use a variety of strategies and activities, such as brainstorming, listing, discussion, drawing, role-playing, note-taking, and journal writing, for finding and developing ideas about which to write.

8. Write to synthesize information from multiple sources.

9. Use figurative language, such as simile, metaphor, and analogies to expand meaning.

10. Revise content, organization, and other aspects of writing, using self, peer, and teacher collaborative feedback (the shared responses of others).

11. Edit writing for developmentally appropriate syntax, spelling, usage, and punctuation.

12. Publish writing in a variety of formats.

13. Establish and use criteria for self and group evaluation of written products.

14. Develop a portfolio or collection of writings.